DINOSAUR DAYS
IGUANODON

HEIGHT: 16' (4.9 M)

HEIGHT: 5' (1.5 M)

DINOSAUR DAYS
IGUANODON

SARA GILBERT
CREATIVE EDUCATION   CREATIVE PAPERBACKS

Table of Contents

Meet *Iguanodon*!	8
First Finds	11
European Adventure	14
Large and Lumbering	17
Timeline	18
Living Large	20
Mysterious End	23
Glossary	24
Read More	24
Websites	24
Index	24

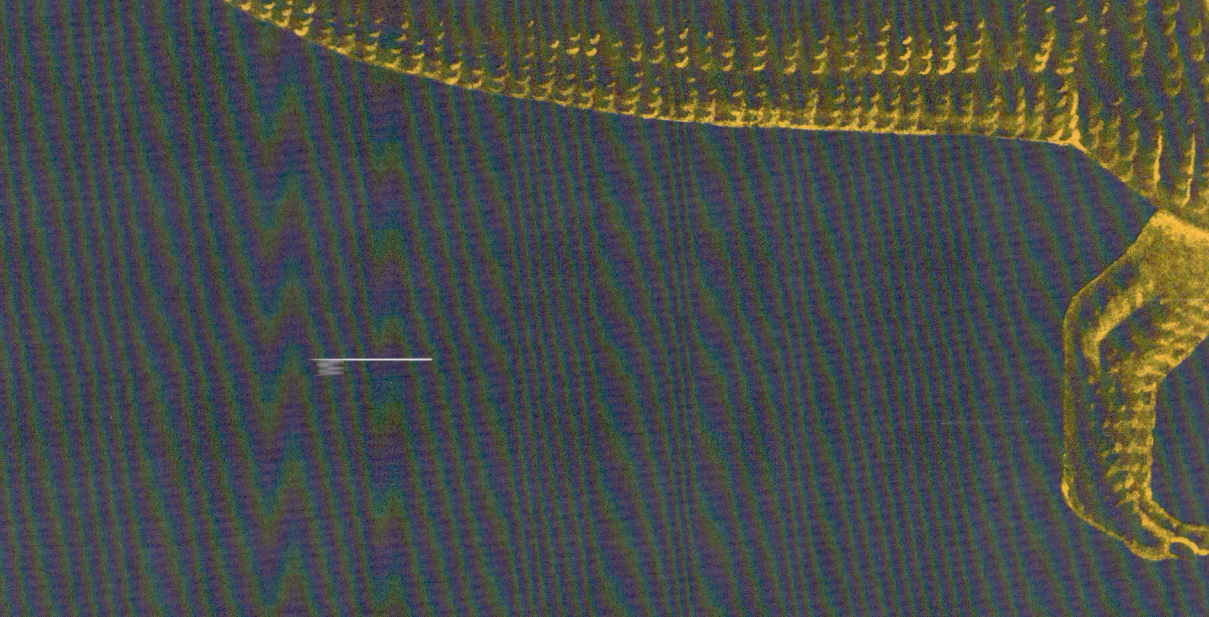

Dinosaur Days — Iguanodon

Published by Creative Education
and Creative Paperbacks
P.O. Box 227, Mankato,
Minnesota 56002
Creative Education and Creative
Paperbacks are imprints of
The Creative Company
www.thecreativecompany.us

Book design by Blue Design
(www.bluedes.com)
Art direction by Rita Marshall
Printed in the United States of America

Photographs by Alamy (Steve Vidler), Creative Commons Wikimedia (O. C. Marsh), Royal Belgian Institute of Natural Sciences (Gustave Lavalette/RBINS/Museum of Natural Sciences), Thinkstock (chronicler101, CoreyFord, Dorling Kindersley, dottedhippo, Elenarts, leonello, paylessimages, Graham Rosewarne, Vac1, Warpaintcobra)

Copyright © 2019 Creative Education, Creative Paperbacks International copyright reserved in all countries. No part of this book may be reproduced in any form without written permission from the publisher.

Library of Congress Cataloging-in-Publication Data
Names: Gilbert, Sara, author.
Title: Iguanodon / Sara Gilbert.
Series: Dinosaur days.

Includes bibliographical references and index.
Summary: This introductory exploration uncovers the discovery of *Iguanodon* fossils before revealing information about its era, features, and lifestyle, as well as its eventual extinction.
Identifiers: ISBN 978-1-64026-047-4 (hardcover) / ISBN 978-1-62832-635-2 (pbk) / ISBN 978-1-64000-163-3 (eBook)

This title has been submitted for CIP processing under LCCN 2018938974.

CCSS: RI.1.1, 2, 4, 5, 6, 7; RI.2.1, 2, 5, 6, 7; RI.3.1, 2, 5, 7; RF.1.1, 3, 4; RF.2.3, 4

First Edition HC 9 8 7 6 5 4 3 2 1
First Edition PBK 9 8 7 6 5 4 3 2 1

Meet *Iguanodon*!

Welcome to the Sedgwick Museum of Earth Sciences. This is part of Cambridge University in England. An *Iguanodon* **skeleton** is near the front door.

The word dinosaur *was first used in 1842—20 years after the first remains of such creatures were discovered.*

Dinosaur Days — **Iguanodon**

10

First Finds

Iguanodon **fossils** were found in England in 1822. Gideon Mantell named it in 1825. It was just the second dinosaur to be named. In 1878, coal miners in Belgium found more bones. There were more than 30 skeletons in the mine!

SCIENTISTS FIRST THOUGHT *IGUANODON* WALKED ON ALL FOURS AND LOOKED LIKE A LIZARD.

Dinosaur Days — Iguanodon

12

Iguanodon — **First Finds**

European Adventure

Iguanodon roamed Europe. It has been found in many places. It lived during the late Jurassic and early Cretaceous periods. *Brachiosaurus* lived in the late Jurassic, too.

> **SOUND-IT-OUT:**
> *Brachiosaurus:*
> *BRACK-ee-uh-SAWR-us*

THE *IGUANODON* FOSSILS FROM THE BELGIAN COAL MINE WERE ALMOST ENTIRELY COMPLETE.

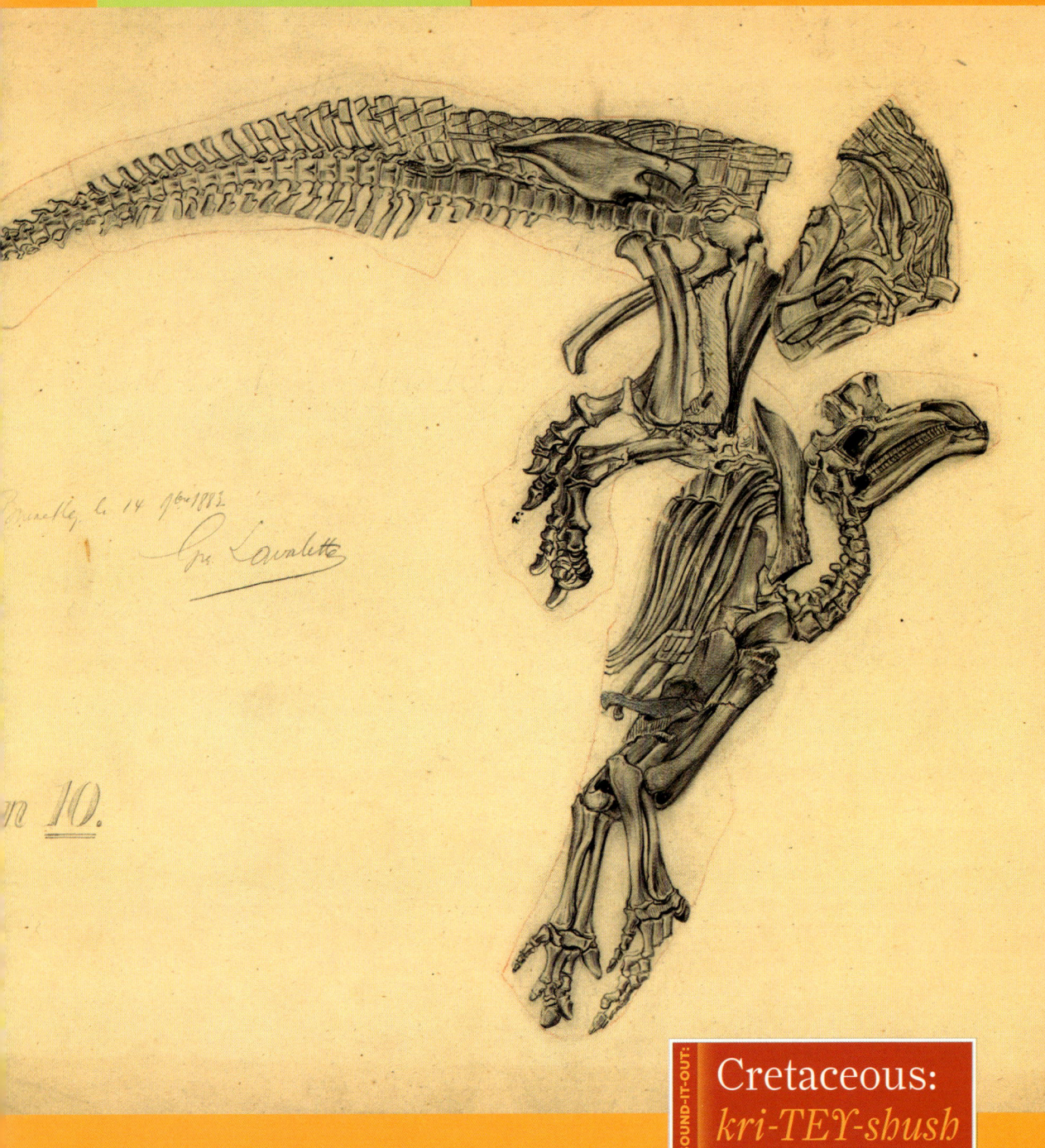

SOUND-IT-OUT: Cretaceous: *kri-TEY-shush*

IGUANODON — European Adventure

15

***IGUANODON* USED ITS SHARP BEAK TO TEAR PLANTS; ITS TEETH CRUSHED THE FOOD.**

Dinosaur Days — **Iguanodon**

16

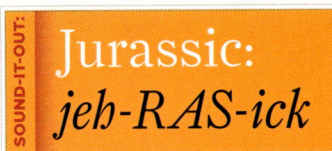

SOUND-IT-OUT: Jurassic: *jeh-RAS-ick*

Large and Lumbering

Bulky *Iguanodon* stood 16 feet (4.9 m) tall. It was as heavy as 5 tons (4.5 t). With its stiff tail, it was longer than 30 feet (9.1 m). Scientists are not sure if it walked on its back legs or on all four legs.

Its front legs had four fingers. Its thumbs were like spikes. It might have used these to grab food. Sharp teeth filled the sides of its mouth. The front of its mouth curved like a bird's beak.

227 MILLION YEARS AGO
LATE TRIASSIC

205 MILLION YEARS AGO
EARLY JURASSIC

180 MILLION YEARS AGO
MID-JURASSIC

Timeline

IGUANODON LIVED HERE!

159 MILLION YEARS AGO
LATE JURASSIC

144 MILLION YEARS AGO
EARLY CRETACEOUS

98 MILLION YEARS AGO
LATE CRETACEOUS

Living Large

Iguanodon ate plants. It could reach tree branches. It could also bend low to eat grass.

Iguanodon was probably hunted by meat-eating dinosaurs. It might have used its thumbs to fight. It may have lived in **herds**. They could have helped each other fight off **predators**.

Iguanodon *was named for its teeth, which look like those of an iguana.*

Iguanodon — Living Large

21

FOSSILS OF *IGUANODON* RELATIVES HAVE BEEN FOUND AROUND THE WORLD.

Dinosaur Days — Iguanodon

22

Mysterious End

During the mid-Cretaceous, *Iguanodon* died out. No one knows exactly what happened. Someday, maybe new clues will tell us why they are gone!

Glossary

fossils — bones or plants preserved for millions of years

herds — groups of animals that live together

predators — animals that hunt other animals for food

skeleton — the bones that support a body

Read More

Lee, Sally. *Iguanodon*. Mankato, Minn.: Capstone Press, 2015.

Rober, Harold T. *Iguanodon*. Minneapolis: Lerner, 2017.

Index

Brachiosaurus	14
Cretaceous	14, 23
Europe	11, 14
food	17, 20
fossils	11
herds	20
Jurassic	14
Mantell, Gideon	11
physical features	17, 20
predators	20
Sedgwick Museum of Earth Sciences	8
size	17

Websites

DK Find Out!: Iguanodon
https://www.dkfindout.com/us/dinosaurs-and-prehistoric-life/dinosaurs/iguanodon/
See a diagram of *Iguanodon*, and take a dinosaur quiz!

National Geographic Kids: Iguanodon
https://kids.nationalgeographic.com/animals/iguanodon/#iguandodon.jpg
Read more about *Iguanodon* and other dinosaurs!